WORDS OF PRAISE FOR

M000028189

Education does not occur until learning takes place. As well as anyone I've known, Jonathan Thigpen understood and practiced this concept. He worked very hard at using the most effective methods to convey information to his students and audiences. He was always attentive to make sure his audiences were "receiving" what he was "sending."

FRANK BREEDEN
Friend and Co-Worker

Jonathan Thigpen was a master story-teller; as you read this book that will be obvious! What may not be so noticeable is how his stories draw you deeper into classic and current theory; broaden your understanding of application to a variety of ministry settings; and raise your confidence in handling and loving the Word of God! The guidelines for using case studies, small groups, discussion and of course—story-telling will greatly assist you. Understanding the unique needs and roles of adults will intrigue you. The chapters are easy to read and make it easy to miss and appreciate the ministry of this wise Christian educator.

DR. GREGORY C. CARLSON
Chair and Professor of Christian Ministries
Trinity International University
Author of *Understanding Teaching and Rock Solid Teacher.*
Chair of the Board of Evangelical Training Association

In a day when godly, strong biblical teachers are needed, this tool will assist you to clearly communicate the life-changing truth of God's word. Whether you teach in small or large groups with younger or older students you will benefit from this material. Teachers, read this slowly, prayerfully, and let's teach God's Word to the next generation!

J. MICHAEL BROYLES, DRE
Grace Baptist Church
Family Life Pastor

This practical book will prove helpful to all Bible teachers, including parents, Sunday school teachers and church leaders. It is based on sound educational and biblical theory, but it is written in such a way that all will be able to benefit from it.

DENNIS WILLIAMS
Distinguished Senior Professor of Leadership and Church Ministry
The Southern Baptist Theological Seminary Executive Administrator,
North American Professors of Christian Education

"We are privileged to get this glimpse of what was important to Jonathan. In terms of education, he was extremely principled and well-established philosophically. These chapters help the rest of us join him in the fulfillment of his vision for teaching students effectively."

STEVEN KEMP
Academic Dean, Antioch School of Church Planting
and Leadership Development
Board Member, Evangelical Training Association
Board Member, Trainers of Pastors International Coalition

This book is a little taste of what it was like to have Jonathan Thigpen as a professor at Free Will Baptist Bible College in the early 80's. I didn't know it then, but I realize now that I was sitting at a buffet table everyday with him in class. At a time when youth ministry was in it's infancy as a viable ministry, Jonathan was able to gaze into the future and see that long term, holistic ministry was built upon a strong Christian Education foundation, whether with adults, teens, or children. What is taught in this book and in the classes I had with him are timeless and profitable for anyone, anywhere who wants to impact students with the Word. Learn these principles and pass it on to help others begin to eat the "meat" of God's Word.

ALLEN POINTER
Youth Pastor
First Free Will Baptist Church, Russellville, Arkansas

Jonathan offers the perfect mix of principle and practicalness in this timeless book for teachers.

STAN TOLER
Pastor of Trinity Church of the Nazarene in Oklahoma City
Author of ReThink Your Life and seventy more.

Within the pages of this book the reader will learn the foundation and skills that make up a creative Bible Teacher. Jonathan reminds us that the goal of the teacher is to change lives. It is tremendous that he left us these great tools to continue the ministry God called Jonathan to do.

KEITH KENEMER
Friend

TEACHING
STUDENTS
not LESSONS

BY

JONATHAN THIGPEN

randall house

114 Bush Rd I Nashville, TN 37217
randallhouse.com

Teaching Students Not Lessons

© 2009 by Jonathan Thigpen

Published by Randall House
114 Bush Road
Nashville, TN 37217

Printed in the United States of America

10-ISBN 0892655550

13-ISBN 9780892655557

www.randallhouse.com

TABLE OF CONTENTS

FOREWORD

BY RON HUNTER, JR.

JONATHAN THOUGHT DIFFERENTLY. He inspired his students to rise above the status quo. It has been said by many that Jonathan Thigpen was a generation ahead of his time. I recently uncovered some writings of his that have never been published in a book and realized how practical they would still be for teachers today. Evangelical Training Association (ETA) contributed three chapters from the last book Jonathan wrote to round out the material contained in this book. Being Jonathan is one of my heroes, I chose to be the general editor of this work and set out to insure that all the writing was in today's vernacular and updated where needed. I quickly discovered that it was not Jonathan who needed to be updated but our own approach to teaching. I am sure in the following pages that Jonathan will challenge you as much as he did those he influenced during his life.

Reading his words will inspire you to approach your class with a whole new outlook. I can still hear Jonathan the professor, the preacher, the consultant, and the teacher of teachers. Jonathan reminds us of what the bible has to say about teaching followed by some proven helps that no teacher should overlook. You may have missed out on hearing Jonathan's teachings personally and while that is tragic, it is more tragic for your students not to get the very best you have to offer them in and out of the classroom.

You may wonder what more you can do and why you should do it. Jonathan told the following story adapted from a story written by Loren Eiseley. Early one morning, man was walking on the beach where literally thousands of starfish had washed up during high tide and as the tide was going back out the starfish were stranded on the shore. The man was picking up the starfish one at the time and throwing them back deep into the ocean so they would not be trapped out of the water long enough to die in the heat of the rising sun. Another man approaching from the other direction noticed what he was doing and commented, "You are wasting your time. There are miles of starfish along the beach; you can't possibly make a difference. Why are you doing this?" The first man hearing the comments bent over and picked up another starfish and held it up and then threw it back into the water replying to the skeptical man, "It made a difference for that one."

Some teachers prepare lessons for one student while others classes are full. Why do teachers prepare? What drives us to study harder? Our students is the answer and because God's Word changes students. That is why we teach student not lessons.

REFLECTIONS ON THE LIFE OF JONATHAN N. THIGPEN

BY YVONNE THIGPEN

THE BOOK OF JOSHUA served as inspiration and guidance for what would be the life of Jonathan Noel Thigpen. Jonathan's journey reflected many of Joshua's themes; reliance on God's strength, the conquering devotion of a Godly warrior, the vivid imagery in communication, and the wooing encouragement of its wisdom. Jonathan loved the dramatic and triumphant spirit of that book.

Jonathan was born in Nashville, Tennessee to Charles and Laura Thigpen on December 17, 1951. He accepted Christ at the tender age of five. The Holy Spirit used a vividly written childhood storybook, read by his mother at bedtime, to bring Jonathan salvation. The impact of that story would not only mark his conversion experience but also cement storytelling as an art form characteristic in Jonathan's communication style for the remainder of his life.

As a young boy his analytical skills were honed in the Thigpen household through closely observing the equally remarkable lives and ministries of his parents. His mother nurtured his creativity and sense of adventure while his father served as an exemplary model of dedication to mission, perseverance and pastoral care. His formative years also provided a close acquaintance with college campus life since both parents taught at Free Will Baptist Bible College. Jonathan learned the routines of professorship as well as the mischievousness of residence life. Campus students were eager to give an audience to his earliest forays into performance, unofficially surrounding Mrs. Laura Thigpen's drama productions. His three younger sisters also enjoyed his comedic sense of humor. Yet, there was a serious nature about young Jonathan that cultivated responsibility and care for his family during Mr. Charles Thigpen's many preaching travels. Nevertheless, Jonathan struck a healthy balance between playfulness and duty through his expertise in sports. Early ambitions in football took a backseat in high school while he excelled on the track. During his college years, intramural football and basketball teammates often bowed their hulking physiques to his shorter but speedier frame as only sportsman comrades can appreciate.

Like all adolescents of the late 1960s, Jonathan wrestled with the tumultuous culture around him and once again drew encouragement from Joshua's declaration "choose whom you will serve." He accepted the call to preach at the age of 15 and served in his teens as plenary speaker for youth camps, church events, and the FWB National Youth Conference. One summer during college, Jonathan stepped outside the confines of the bible college environment to open a coffee house ministry where the street people of Nashville could safely come and converse about faith. Some of the converts of that season still serve the Lord; even reaching the foreign mission field.

Jonathan was a ministerial student while at Free Will Baptist Bible College. He won a celebrated sermon contest as a student and demonstrated many other leadership superlatives. His most memorable creation, with two close friends Vernon and Rodney Whaley, was formation of *The Conquerors* evangelistic team. Together they traveled to churches across the country sharing creative drama presentations, youthful Christian music, and Jonathan's unique preaching; styled with the vibrant imagery and motivation he learned studying Joshua.

"For me and my house, we will serve the Lord," was the cornerstone of his marriage to Yvonne, who was not only became his life partner but also his professional colleague. The same characteristics Jonathan learned in his childhood were imparted to his daughter Jessica. Teaching God's Word was a passion in his own home as Jonathan embraced every opportunity as a teachable moment.

In his 35 year career he fulfilled many roles; youth worker, evangelist, pastor, publishing executive, and writer. None of the positions was any more loved than the role of teacher. He realized an opportunity to commemorate great milestones for the FWB Foreign Missions Department and Randall House Publications by leading their key celebrations with a multi-media presentation (challenging for the times) on the national platform. When technology further allowed the means to video record the National Convention, it was Jonathan who stepped up to prove this living history documentation could be done. When curriculum development needed a boost, he incorporated innovative learning styles into a newly published product line. Jonathan later replicated his motivational spirit in the college classroom, on the same campus where he once romped as a boy. The appreciation he enjoyed as a campus mascot, he came to enjoy again as a favored teacher and mentor.

Jonathan's joy in teaching and striving for excellence in service took him to Tennessee Temple Seminary to earn his Master's in Religious Education. There he refined skills for the lifelong adult learner. He pastored a small congregation during those study years at Hixon Free Will Baptist Church. That small congregation formed a foundational understanding for the years ahead when his attention would turn to the vast needs of church volunteers. He was able to contribute significantly to Evangelical Training Association while serving as its President from 1992-2001. During that period he completed his Ph.D. at Trinity Evangelical Divinity School in Deerfield, Illinois.

The greatest challenge of his life, and perhaps his greatest opportunity to demonstrate the power of Christ upon a single individual, came in late 1995 when Jonathan was diagnosed with ALS, commonly called Lou Gehrig's disease. Miraculously and mercifully, God allowed Jonathan to continue his ministry until the day of his death in May 2001. The last years were naturally the most reflective. He was able to revisit all the teaching techniques of his ministry and leave them as a legacy for others. When sharing his tips for effectively teaching he loved to tell an anecdote from one of his mentor's, Campbell Wycoff. "Cam, he once asked, "What do you believe about the ministry of the Holy Spirit in teaching?" Campbell replied, "Jonathan, I believe the Holy Spirit *is* the teacher, and we are simply teacher's aides." Jonathan would hasten to emphasize, "If I learned nothing else from that gentleman but that truth, my life would have been enriched."

In one of Jonathan's final public addresses, he left his colleagues with three thoughts that serve us all well: "First, don't lose your passion for what's happening in the local church. A heartbeat and passion for what is happening in the Sunday school class and the youth group, and the kids club…don't let that slip. Secondly, don't just strive to be a great teacher; strive to become a great trainer of teachers. And finally, finish well. It is one thing to start well, but I want to *finish* well." And so he did.

CHAPTER 1

SIX LEVELS
OF LEARNING

THE STORY is told about a businessman who noticed some unusual telephone poles as he was driving along back country roads. For about two miles before he entered the city limit, the poles on each side of the road were decorated with large black and white bull's-eyes, each with a bullet hole dead in the center of the target. After seeing scores of such poles, each with a perfect shot in the center of the target, the man pulled into the town's only gas station to inquire of the expert marksman. When he asked the attendant the name of the town sharpshooter, the man replied, "Why, that's Crazy Harry." "Crazy Harry?" the traveler replied. "What's so crazy about being able to shoot that well?"

"Well, you see," came the answer, because he always shoots the telephone pole first, and then he paints the bull's-eye."

We would all agree that to shoot first and then paint a target is certainly not the way to determine who is the best shot. This same principle is true in teaching as well. The only way for us to aim properly as teachers is for us to aim at the right target. However, many teachers are much like Crazy Harry; they aim at nothing and they are usually very good at hitting it.

When we think of what we want to accomplish in our Sunday School teaching, we need to ask ourselves each Sunday, "What do I want the Lord to do in the lives of my students as a result of this lesson?" Do we really have a clear view of what we want to see accomplished in our 45 minutes of teaching? Unfortunately, if you asked the average Sunday School teacher 30 seconds before walking into the Sunday School room, "What is your goal for the class today?" he would probably respond, "To get through the lesson." If that is the only goal that you have in teaching the Bible, you may be able to accomplish it. But the real question is, "Am I going for the right goal, the really important goal? Are there other goals that I need to keep in mind as I prepare my lesson each week?"

Christian educators, such as Larry Richards and Leroy Ford, proposed a helpful way to view learning. This is true as it happens on different levels whether it occurs in Sunday School or elsewhere, as happening on different levels. This view compares the learning process to climbing a set of stairs. While we think we can leap to the top step, each one is a set of incremental steps. The only way that you can get to the top of the stairs is to begin at the bottom. Thus, when learning is viewed as a stair-step process, learning moves from simple to complex forms of response.

Leroy Ford, in his book, *Design for Teaching and Training* (published by Broadman Press), details six levels of learning that he believes describe the learning process. In this chapter the first three steps will be examined. Understanding the purpose of the steps brings insight in the way you approach your students.

Why is it important to understand the levels of learning? First, a study of the levels of learning emphasizes that learning is more than the mere memorization and recitation of facts. This is certainly part of the learning process, but it is only the beginning, not the ultimate goal of Christian education. Second, a study of learning levels clarifies the higher levels of learning that Sunday School teachers should be aiming for in their lessons. Third, learning levels are important because they will also suggest various methods that can be used in helping our students reach the highest levels of learning.

FIRST STEP—KNOWLEDGE

The previous chart illustrates the first three levels of learning. The first is the KNOWLEDGE level. This is the basic level of all learning at which the learner's role is to memorize and recall facts by rote memory. At this level, the pupil does not even need to understand what is being learned. For example, learning on this level takes place when a student is led to memorize John 3:16. For John 3:16 to be learned on the KNOWLEDGE level, all a student has to do is to repeat, word-for-word, the verse. This level of learning is certainly important for without the basic knowledge of the facts of Scripture, a person could not even be saved. However, our learning must progress beyond this level if we are going to be transformed by the Word of God. The tragedy is, a person could memorize John 3:16 letter perfect, know it backwards and forward, and still die unprepared to meet God. Scripture memorization is foundational and as a result it is not the highest level of learning and by itself does not produce spiritual growth.

To understand this level of learning in more depth, read carefully each of the following statements and choose which one represents the KNOWLEDGE level of learning:

___Lead my students to apply Scriptural principles to their daily lives.

___Lead my students in memorizing Psalm 23.

___Help my students set up a daily devotional time.

If you chose the second statement, then you see that to "apply" or to "set up" goes beyond just memorizing the words of Scripture. Again, this level is certainly important and it cannot be bypassed, but teachers who only aim for their students to memorize and playback the right words are aiming at the wrong target.

SECOND STEP—COMPREHENSION

The second of Ford's levels is that of COMPREHENSION. This level goes beyond mere memorization and involves the student in putting the facts that he or she has learned into his or her own language. Richards refers to this level of learning as the "restatement" level. Ford adds that this level is where the student is also able to explain how one idea relates to another one. Read the statements below, and check the one that contains lesson aims for the COMPREHENSION level of learning:

___Teach so my students can paraphrase the Bible story to their parents.

___Challenge my students to memorize this week's key verse.

___Guide my students in applying the principles of Psalm 1 to their relationships with other people.

If you choose the first statement, you have a grasp of what the COMPREHENSION level is all about. If you were teaching John 3:16, you might ask the students to put in their own words what the verse means to them. In order to do this, the student has to go beyond memorizing the words without thought of their meaning, and must think in terms of exactly what the words of the verse actually mean. This level still does not guarantee that an individual has personally responded to the truth of the verse but rather that the person is gaining a fuller understanding of its meaning. The second statement emphasizes learning at the KNOWLEDGE level. The last statement deals with the next level of learning, the APPLICATION level.

THIRD STEP—APPLICATION

The APPLICATION level of learning goes beyond the first two and suggests the ability of the student to apply a principle or truth that has been learned in a new and different situation. Ford calls this process the "transfer of learning." For example, let's suppose that you are teaching Romans 3, where Paul presents his case for the sinfulness of all men.

A student could memorize Romans 3:23 and even paraphrase it. A student could even give a theologically sound definition of sin and yet not make the connection that he personally is a sinner before God and accountable to Him. When the student reaches the APPLICATION level, he goes beyond the first two steps of just what a passage of Scripture says and what that passage means to the ability to apply that Scripture to himself or herself and others.

This same student, after studying Romans 3, might be confronted with the thought of the spiritual condition of people in third world countries while watching a news report on television. Although the teacher in the Sunday School did not specifically say anything about the "heathen," but the student who has progressed to the APPLICATION level of learning is able to figure out that Romans 3 applies to them as well and that they are people in need of becoming followers of Christ.

Choose the statement below that best characterizes the APPLICATION level of learning:

___Ask my students to explain the meaning of John 3:16.

___Lead my students in a discussion of how John 3:16 can be communicated to lost people.

___To read three verses and ask my students to identify which one is John 3:16.

The second statement is the only one that deals with the APPLICATION level of learning. The first simply asks for meaning, the third asks only for the ability to recognize what has been memorized, but the second statement requires that the students give some serious thought as to how the message of John 3:16 can be shared with those who need to be saved. To come up with the correct answer, the student cannot rely on some fact previously memorized or on simply restating what he already knows, but he must forge ideas and thoughts into areas that are unknown with the truths that students has already learned. Students must apply the truths of Scripture by themselves to solve a problem they are facing.

As you review these first three levels of learning—KNOWLEDGE, COMPREHENSION, and APPLICATION—ask yourself on what level you are teaching. For what level are you aiming each week as you teach you class?

All three of these levels are important and none of them should be ignored, and yet it is clear that real change cannot occur in a person's life until personal application of the truths of God's Word is practiced. As a Sunday School teacher, you serve as a catalyst in this process. You should do all that you can to encourage higher levels of learning and personal response to the unchanging truths of the Word of God.

SELECT BIBLIOGRAPHY

Bloom, Benjamin, ed. *Taxonomy of Educational Objectives, Handbook 1: Cognitive Domain,* New York: David McKay Co., Inc., 1956.

Ford, Leroy. *Design for Teaching and Training,* Nashville: Broadman Press, 1978.

Richards, Lawrence. *Creative Bible Teaching,* Chicago: Moody Press, 1970.

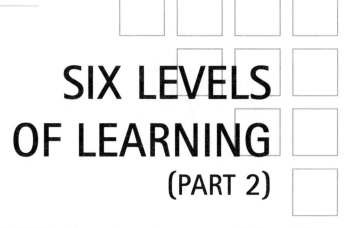

CHAPTER 2

SIX LEVELS
OF LEARNING
(PART 2)

GOOD TEACHING is like good target shooting; you will always do better when you are aiming at the bull's eye. Unfortunately, many teachers do not accomplish what they would like to because they are either not aiming at the bull's-eye, or they are aiming at the wrong target altogether.

In the last chapter, we discussed the first three of Leroy Ford's six "levels of learning." These levels are to the Bible teacher what the target is to the marksman on the rifle range. The first three levels of learning are the *knowledge* level (simple recall of facts or rote memorization); the *comprehension* level (the ability to express ideas in your own words); and the *application* level (the ability to relate truths to one's own life). While all of these three levels are important and necessary in the learning process, they do not represent the final aim of teaching.

FOURTH STEP—ANALYSIS

The fourth level of learning is the **ANALYSIS** level. This is the level of learning in which the student undertakes and executes problem solving. The first three steps are all necessary tools in the problem solving process. The student takes a fact that he has learned, states it in his own language, comprehends a personal application, and then relates it to a new situation.

For example, the student has learned that it is wrong to think evil thoughts. He has memorized verses that deal with this and is able to put the principle into his own words; he understands that evil thoughts are sinful. In the application stage, he goes a step further and realizes that it is wrong for him to think evil thoughts. Then, he is confronted one day by a magazine at a friend's home or a barbershop. As he flips through the pages, he immediately realizes that something is wrong. Although this process is almost instantaneous, he analyzes the situation based on the facts at his disposal and his comprehension and application of them, and he suddenly realizes that to continue looking at this particular magazine would be sinful.

FIFTH STEP—ASSIMILATION

The fifth level is yet a higher, more complex teaching goal, the *assimilation* level. At this level, the student is able to take all that he has learned up to this point and put it together in a way that is new to him. For example, he may take the truths on thinking impure thoughts and build a brief devotional around them to present to his Sunday School class. He must work through the first four levels to get to this point, but by now, he not only owns this truth, but this truth owns him. Assimilation is more than simply parroting what someone else has said; it is the organizing and integrating of the truth so that it can be communicated through the life of the learner. He is now living the truth not merely learning it.

SIXTH STEP—EVALUATION

The sixth level of learning is the *evaluation* stage. According to Ford, this is the highest level of learning and the one at which Bible teachers should aim. At this level, the student is able to make value judgments and decisions based on all that has been learned in the previous levels. Decisions are made not on the basis of what the teacher thinks but rather what the student now thinks in light of the Word of God. At this level, the student can effectively deal with issues involving values and standards. The student can decide not only the *what* but also the *why* of his actions.

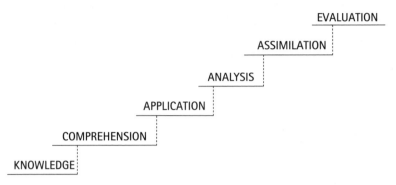

How can these upper three levels be reached? Each of them requires a slightly different approach. The analysis level can be stimulated and reached through the use of problem solving activities. Open-ended case studies and true-life stories can be shared with the pupils, so that they are left with the opportunity to decide what should or should not be done. The student should also be given chances to organize what has been taught into an outline or other form that is meaningful to him. The answers should not be spoon-fed from the teacher to the student, but rather the student should be given room to grow and expand his own problem-solving skills.

The *assimilation* level can be encouraged by giving the student an opportunity to present his own research in a classroom setting. The teacher gives the assignment; the student does his own research and then must understand it and organize it sufficiently for the rest of the class to comprehend. In this type of activity, invariably, the student presenting a report will always learn the most from it. This is a result from the assimilation level of learning that must be reached if the student is going to fulfill the assignment.

The *evaluation* level is at once both the easiest level and the hardest level to achieve. It is the easiest because it is so easy to confuse proper evaluative skills with one's own prejudice and preference. Adults usually respond well to discussion of values and standards, but a lively discussion is no sign that the evaluation level has been reached. Incorrect interpretation discussion does not advance one's learning. Thus, it is the hardest level to stimulate because it must be based on the pupil progressing through the first five levels. Adults should be asked not only to explain their values but the "whys" behind their values. They must not only stand up for their own standards but explain from a Biblical perspective, "not personal" why they hold them. The teacher cannot always tell when this or any level has been achieved, but it should certainly be the teacher's goal to do all he or she can to facilitate student achievement of the highest level.

SUMMARY

An improving teacher is one who is willing to carefully evaluate his teaching ministry in light of what God expects him to do.

As you prepare your next small group or Sunday School lesson, keep these questions in mind to help you develop models to achieve the highest levels of learning in your teaching.

1. What are the facts that the students need to know in this lesson? How can I present the facts in a creative, attractive way?

2. What opportunities can I give my student for feedback and for expressing the truths of the lesson in their own words?

3. What illustrations can I share or questions can I ask to assure that the students fully understand all the applications and implications of the lesson?

4. What problems can I suggest that need to be solved and can be solved by applying the truths of this lesson?

5. What can the learner discover from this lesson that can apply to other areas of his life? How can this lesson help the student in his home life, work life, school life, etc.

6.   For what values or standards does this passage lay the foundation? What principle can I discover in this passage that can help the student make wiser decisions?

An improving teacher is one who is willing to carefully evaluate his or her teaching ministry in light of what God expects him or her to do. These six levels of learning are simply ways to help the teacher understand the steps that are involved in fulfilling the Great Commission. The maturing Bible teacher will agree with apostle Paul when he wrote, " . . . this mystery, which is Christ in you, the hope of glory. We proclaim him, admonishing and teaching everyone with all wisdom; so that we may present everyone perfect in Christ. To this end I labor, struggling with all his energy, which so powerfully works in me." (Colossians 1:27-29)

CHAPTER 3

BIBLICAL BASIS OF CHRISTIAN EDUCATION

EVERYONE CELEBRATES when a child is born. But by the time the child arrives home, the reality will sink in that the journey of this couple as parents has just begun. The nine months of waiting becomes a short time compared to the years of responsibility of parenting this child to live in the world as an adult. Preparing to be a parent is dramatically different from a parent preparing a child. The process of conception, fetal development, and birth is certainly important; however, more important is the process of nurturing and developing the child to maturity. God loans us our children for only a short portion of their lives.

This same truth applies to the spiritual realm. The new birth is of crucial importance. Yet it is only the beginning of a process that continues throughout life. Personal salvation is the beginning of a process that is designed to culminate in the Christian's being "conformed to the likeness of his Son" (Romans 8:29). Christian education is that part of the church's ministry that is concerned with the spiritual growth of those who have been born again. One of the clearest New Testament passages dealing with this is Matthew 28:18-20, the "Great Commission." The main verbal command in the passage is "teach all nations," literally, "make disciples of all peoples." The process of making disciples includes the other three variables: going into all the world, baptizing converts in the name of the triune God, and then "teaching them to obey everything." Of the three, the "teaching" them involves the greatest investment of time, energy, and a plan.

Then it is clear that the command to "make disciples" has not been fulfilled until those who have been converted have been taught the commandments of Jesus. Disciple-making is not completed when a person make a public profession of faith and is baptized; it can be fulfilled only through Christian education.

Exactly what is Christian education? Most would recognize the Sunday School as part of Christian education, and many would throw in children's church and youth ministry. Someone else may view Christian education as only what goes on in the Christian day school, and another may view it as the specialized training. But listing the ministries of the local church does not actually define Christian education.

DEFINING CHRISTIAN EDUCATION

First, one must define the term "education." I would define it as "the process of change that happens as a person interacts with his environment." Education is concerned with all of the ways a human being changes. Then Christian education is a specific area of education that with the changes in a human being regarding their relationship to Jesus Christ.

This chart represents a concise, comprehensive, definition of Christian education, naming eight essentials that will be discussed in the following section.

DEFINITION OF CHRISTIAN EDUCATION

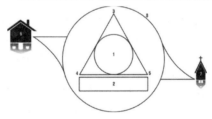

A process of change that is . . .

1) Christ centered	Colossians 1:18
2) Bible based	2 Timothy 3:16, 17
3) Teacher led	2 Timothy 2:2
4) Pupil involved	Proverbs 1:7
5) Life related	Proverbs 3:6
6) Home focused	Deuteronomy 6:6, 7
	Ephesians 6:4
7) Local church directed	1 Timothy 3:5
8) Holy Spirit empowered and controlled	Colossians 1:28, 29

. . . that produces spiritually maturing Christians.

BIBLICAL BASIS OF CHRISTIAN EDUCATION

While Christian education is concerned with organization, methods, and materials, its heart is based on the command of our Lord to teach our converts. First, then, Christian education is education that is committed to the Lord Jesus Christ and the need of all human beings to know Him personally. Christ should have the first place in all things (Colossians 1:18). Wherever true Christian education is practiced, Jesus Christ is Lord of the process.

Second, Christian education is Bible based. The Christ at the center is the Christ of the infallible and inerrant Scriptures. Roy Zuck states, "Without the Bible as the foundation and core of the curriculum, there can be no true Christian education."[1] Paul challenges us when he told Timothy about the power of scripture in that it is from the breath of God and the benefits are for teaching, correction, and training. (2 Timothy 3:16, 17)

Third, Christian education is a process led by a teacher. Ultimately the Holy Spirit is the teacher, but God has chosen to use human teachers to assist in maturing the saints. In the broad sense, every believer is to be a teacher. (Colossians 3:16) All parents, for example, are to be teachers of the Word of God to their children. (Deuteronomy 6:3-9; Ephesians 6:4) God has given to some believers the gift of teaching which they are to use to build up the body of Christ. (Romans 12:6, 7)

Fourth, Christian education can take place only when the pupil is involved. One of the purposes of Proverbs was to give instruction. (Proverbs 1:4) A truth mentioned often in Proverbs is that in order for a person to learn, the basic prerequisite is the inward attitude of fearing God: "The fear of the LORD is the beginning of knowledge: but fools despise wisdom and discipline" (Proverbs 1:7). In order for the learner to mature spiritually, he must manifest the "fear of the LORD." Although teachers must do all they can to promote this attitude and encourage its development, the crucial choice is with the learner.

Fifth, Christian education must be related to the real life needs of the pupil. If the lives of people are going to be changed, the Word of God must be taught in such a way that its meaning is relevant to their daily needs. Proverbs, again, is a good example of life-related teaching; the writer is vitally concerned with the daily activities of the readers. True Christian education is never limited merely to what the Bible says, but is always concerned with what the Bible means and how it applies to everyday life.

Sixth, the home is the focal point of Christian education. The Scriptures make this clear. The "Shema" is what the Jewish people call Deuteronomy 6:3-9 and consider it the foundational educational command given by God to teach their kids. This passage challenges parents to know the Word of God for themselves and to diligently teach it to their children. Paul, in Ephesians 6 commands the father to raise his children in the "instruction of the Lord." Christian education in the local church should focus on helping Christian parents to do "Christian education" at home.

Seventh, the program of Christian education should be directed by the local church. While the church cannot take over the parents' responsibility to teach their children the things of God, it is true that God has ordained the local church as the context in which spiritual gifts are to be exercised for the purpose of building up the body of Christ. In Ephesians 4:7-16, Paul wrote concerning spiritual gifts and the reason they were given. The primary place of their functioning is in the local church. Christian education is not something separate or different from the local church; it is the local church practicing its responsibility to "teach all things."

Eighth, Christian education is empowered and controlled by the Holy Spirit. Throughout the New Testament, ministry is pictured as God and man working together. God has chosen us to be "co-laborers" with Him by using His strength that is far more powerful than our own. Paul was a hard worker and realized his responsibility to do his best in the ministry. At the same time, he was humbly aware that the power of God was working through him. Roy Zuck writes:

> *The Holy Spirit, working through the Word of God, is the spiritual dynamic for Christian living. If the Holy Spirit is not at work through the teacher and through the written Word of God, then Christian education remains virtually ineffective and is little different from secular teaching.*[3]

The goal of Christian education is to produce Christians who are spiritually maturing. I say "spiritually maturing" instead of "spiritually mature" because the New Testament does not indicate that the process of Christian education is ever over in this life. Even Paul, late in life, said that he had not "arrived" in a spiritual sense, but was still reaching or pressing on to achieve God's high calling for him (Philippians 3:12-14). With Paul we affirm our goal in presenting Christ is through preaching and teaching with wisdom to help others continue to mature in Christ.

ENDNOTES

[1]Roy Zuck, *Spiritual Power in Your Teaching (Moody, 1963), page 15.*

[2]Werner Graendorf, *Introduction to Biblical Christian Education* (Moody, 1981), page 27.

[3]Zuck; pages 18 and 19.

CHAPTER 4

CHRISTIAN EDUCATION IN TODAY'S CHURCH

THE NEW TESTAMENT not only defines Christian education but also shows how it functions. Two passages give helpful insight. The first is Acts 2:41-42, which summarizes the activity of the church in its early days.

> *Those who accepted his message were baptized, and about three thousand were added to their number that day. They devoted themselves to the apostles' teaching and to the fellowship, to the breaking of bread and to prayer.*

From the very beginning, the early church was concerned with *evangelism, teaching, fellowship, worship*, and *service* (verse 46). These five major elements can be seen throughout Acts.

This says to me that Christian education consists of the local church providing doctrinal teaching, training people to serve, and a context for fellowship; the other two elements, worship and evangelism, are expressed in each of the other three. Worship occurs as Christian education is *God*-conscious; evangelism as it is *man*-conscious. This chart diagrams this.

The Process of C.E. in the Local Church

The second passage that gives special insight into the function of Christian education is Ephesians 4:11-16.

> It was he who gave some to be apostles, some to be prophets, some to be evangelists, and some to be pastors and teachers, to prepare God's people for works of service, so that the body of Christ may be built up until we all reach unity in the faith and in the knowledge of the Son of God and become mature, attaining to the whole measure of the fullness of Christ. Then we will no longer be infants, tossed back and forth by the waves, and blown here and there by every wind of teaching and by the cunning and craftiness of men in their deceitful scheming. Instead, speaking the truth in love, we will in all things grow up into him who is the Head, that is, Christ. From him the whole body, joined and held together by every supporting ligament, grows and builds itself up in love, as each part does its work.

This certainly teaches that Christ has given spiritual gifts to people to be used in the church. However, Paul goes on to describe exactly what these gifted men people are to be doing. Their function in the church is to mature the saints so that they can do the work of the ministry that will result in the building up of the body of Christ.[1] Thus, in this passage, we see the following factors in Christian education.

THE PERSONNEL: Gifted leaders
THE PROCESS: Teaching doctrine; training for service
THE PRODUCT: Maturing, unified, knowing, ministering Christians
THE PURPOSE: Mutual edification; outreach to build Christ's church

Both Acts 2 and Ephesians 4 emphasize the three-fold function of Christian education in the church, which is to provide Christians with spiritual "input" (teaching the Word of God), spiritual "output" (training for service), and spiritual "throughput" (a context of fellowship with other believers). This is pictured in the following chart.

TEACHING STUDENTS NOT LESSONS

The Process of C.E. in the Local Church

All of the organizations involved in the process of Christian education—the Sunday School, small groups, leadership training, children's ministries, the youth program, the children's church, the Christian day school, and others—exist to fulfill one or more of these three functions. When these are in healthy, balanced operation in a local congregation, that church will be worshipping, evangelizing, and growing mature believers.

CHRISTIAN EDUCATION PROBLEMS IN THE AVERAGE CHURCH

Many pastors are aware that the Christian education program in the church is not all that it should be when evaluated by the New Testament. What is the problem? From my personal experience, working in several churches and consulting in travels all over North America there are five common problems.

First, there is often a lack of trained teachers and workers qualified to direct and conduct a healthy Christian education ministry. Admitting this problem is one thing; it is something else to do something constructive, well planned, and Biblical to alleviate the problem.

This leads to a second problem: Many pastors are not knowledgeable in the area of Christian education. If the pastor does not have a clear understanding of what the local church needs to be doing in the area of Christian education and how it can be accomplished, one cannot expect the people in the congregation to rise above their present level.

Third, many people have accepted five common myths about Christian education.

1. Christian education is something that happens magically whenever the Bible is read and preached. The Holy Spirit will teach Christians regardless of the inadequacies of the human teacher.

2. Christian education is something that only happens in Sunday School.

3. Christian education is the church's responsibility. Christian parents should delegate their responsibility in educating their children to the church.

4. Christian education is done only in a Christian day school. If a church has a school, it has fulfilled its responsibility in Christian education.

5. Christian education is something just for children and teenagers.

All of the statements above are either partially or totally incorrect!

A fourth problem is the failure of many churches to provide adequate money in their budgets for the education ministries of the church. Often, Sunday School teachers, youth workers, and others pay from their own pockets to provide needed material and supplies. The church that truly believes in Christian education will not just talk about it but budget for it with the same priorities as other categories.

Fifth, many church buildings are not designed or maintained to support a growing ministry of Christian education. One of the "Seven Laws of Sunday School Growth," states that the church building sets the pattern for growth. The building often sets limitations on the educational ministry of the church. All too often, the church building has not been designed (too few Sunday School rooms) or maintained (unattractive and unequipped) to foster growth. While the best building in the world cannot win people or teach the Word by itself, a poor building can severely limit the people we can win and the effectiveness of the teaching of believers.

SOME CONCLUDING SUGGESTIONS

What we have learned from looking at the problems the average local church faces, leads to five important suggestions.

1. The catalyst for the rebirth of the educational program in any local church lies with the leadership of the pastor.

    All programs of CE (Sunday School, small groups, children, youth, adults) should have cohesion and directed under the Deuteronomy 6, Ephesians 4, and Acts 2 principles.

2. Systematic training programs must be established to provide adequate leadership for current and future Christian education Programs.

3. The pastor must lead his people in allocating money to be spent in the area of Christian education.

4. Careful evaluation should be made of the current educational use of church facilities as well as the needs for future expansion.

The needs of the average church in the area of Christian education are great, but the command of our Lord is clear. Christian education is not an option for the church. It is an absolute necessity if we are to fulfill the great commission. The challenge of the New Testament is for the church to evangelize the world, yes! But it also commands us to educate thoroughly those who are won. May God give us the wisdom to evaluate and structure the educational ministry of the church so that His last command is our first priority.

ENDNOTE

[1]Kenneth Gangel, *Building Leaders for Church Education* (Moody, 1981), pages 29 and 30.

CHAPTER 5

SEVEN LAWS OF TEACHING

IS TEACHING an art or a science? This question has been discussed for centuries and it will probably continue to be so. Those who argue that teaching is an art focus on the personhood of both teacher and learner and contending that it is not possible to scientifically gather and analyze all of the data needed for such an undertaking. Others who argue that teaching is a science compare the teacher to a gardener who must know and apply the laws of horticulture in order to be successful. Perhaps the best position is to recognize that teaching is both an art and a science. This being noted, many educators would argue that there are certain principles (some would call them laws) that can guide the teacher in understanding the processes of teaching and learning as well as the role of the teacher and the place of methodology in those processes.

JOHN MILTON GREGORY

One such educator was John Milton Gregory, an ordained minister, who spent his life working primarily in public education. His crowning work was the organizing of what would become the University of Illinois. In his classic work, *The Seven Laws of Teaching* (first published in 1884, revised in 1954, and still in print), Gregory presents a succinct overview of the important factors governing the processes of teaching and learning.[1] This chapter presents an updated summary of Gregory's seven laws. Although much important educational research has been done in the past century, it has only supported Gregory's basic positions, confirming why they are true.

Some Christian educators may worry that Gregory's approach diminishes the role of the Holy Spirit in the process of Christian education. However, the Holy Spirit is not dishonored by the application of the laws of teaching any more than He is dishonored when people comply with the laws of gravity or horticulture. Dr. D. Campbell Wyckoff expressed it this way when he was asked about the role of the Holy Spirit in Christian education: "The Holy Spirit is the teacher. We are only aides."[2]

As you will discover, Gregory's laws are intuitive and are used by all great teachers whether or not they are consciously aware of them. New teachers will be guided by them, while experienced teachers will gain new insights into their educational practices.

LAW #1—THE LAW OF THE TEACHER: *The teacher must know that which is to be taught.*

The role of the teacher is critical to the learning process. While some things can be learned through experience or self-discovery without the assistance of a teacher, imagine what would happen in both public and Christian education if no teachers taught! A teacher must be prepared to teach. A teacher cannot teach what he or she has not first learned. As a Christian teacher, you must have knowledge in several key areas:

1. *You must know without a doubt that you have a personal, vital and growing relationship with God through His Son, Jesus Christ.* It will be difficult to lead students to know God if you do not have confidence in your own relationship with Him.

2. *You must be a diligent student of the Word of God.* Every Bible teacher should possess an overview of the Bible; an understanding of the origin, inspiration, and canonicity of the Scriptures; and a solid grasp of the basic doctrines of the Bible. In addition, he or she should have a working knowledge of hermeneutics (principles of biblical interpretation) including Bible study methods and tools.

3. *You should possess the spiritual gift of teaching (Romans 12:3-8; 1 Corinthians 12:27-31).* The gift of teaching is the supernatu-

TEACHING STUDENTS NOT LESSONS

ral ability to share the Word of God with others in a way that produces life change. Keep in mind that spiritual gifts are often given in embryonic form. Thus, you have the responsibility to develop your gift of teaching and invest it for the glory of God.

4. *You should be convinced of God's power to change the life of anyone who turns to Him in faith.* As you teach, you are actually teaching two sets of students; your students as they actually are and your students as they can be by God's grace.

5. *You should seek to know everything possible about the students you teach.* You should carefully study the age-group characteristics of your students collectively, as well as their specific needs individually.

6. *You should learn everything possible about becoming a better teacher (which is one of the reasons you are reading this book).* Read good books about teaching. Talk to other teachers about successful techniques and new ideals. Attend workshops that help you become a better teacher.

7. *Never forget that you are a learner too.* You will never reach a place where there is not a new truth or new skill to learn.

LAW #2—THE LAW OF THE LEARNER: *The learner must desire to learn that which is to be taught.*

The educational process demands both a teacher and a learner. If a teacher does not possess certain knowledge, he or she cannot teach effectively. In the same way, a student can become a learner only when he or she desires to do so. Teachers have the responsibility to create an atmosphere in which learning is desirable. To do so, the teacher must capture the attention of students and develop it into an interest for the subject.

1. *Attention.* Attention span is heavily dependent upon the age of the student. Preschool children have very short attention spans, perhaps one minute for each year of age. Primary children will have an increasingly lengthened period of sus-

tained attention. They begin to appreciate their own abilities and to enjoy longer periods of thought or discussion. By the middle of the first grade or during the second, well-trained students begin to make the transition from much physical activity to the enjoyment of mental exercise. Their attention spans become noticeable longer. When teaching these students, involve them in a creative or thought-provoking activity as soon as they arrive to class. If the first activity attracts their attention, you will be better able to keep it throughout the lesson.

2. *Interest.* Sustained attention is dependent on interest. It is easy to gain and hold the attention of an interested student. An imperative command or some clever eye-catching trick may temporarily attract attention, but genuine interest alone will sustain it.

Ability to gain and maintain interest will depend on these factors:

✓ Discovering the student's plane of thought.

✓ Guarding against outside distractions.

✓ Providing a lesson suited to the student's capacity.

✓ Enlisting the student's cooperation in the lesson.

Attention and interest are directly related to motivation. Motivated learning is learning that is desired by the student. To best motivate students to learn, gear the lesson to their needs.

LAW # 3—THE LAW OF THE LANGUAGE: *The language must be common to both teacher and learner.*

It takes more than a prepared teacher and a motivated student for learning to occur. Both teacher and student must be speaking the same language. Missionaries must know the language of the people group they are serving. If the missionary is speaking English and the students only understand Chinese, not much learning can take place. What may be less obvious is that this principle holds true even when the teacher and student are both speaking the same language.

For example, if you are teaching students in grade school or high school, you will probably have a larger vocabulary than the students. To communicate effectively, you must limit yourself to the language of the students. If you fail to adjust to the students' language, you risk a breakdown in communication and comprehension in teaching.

The language will differ for every age and department in the church. Here are some basic guidelines:

1. Study the language of the student constantly and carefully.

2. Discern your students' knowledge of the subject.

3. Express yourself in the language of your students.

4. Use simple and few words to express your meaning.

5. To clarify meaning, repeat your thoughts using different words, if possible with greater simplicity.

6. Use illustrations to aid in the meaning of words.

7. Try to increase the size of the students' vocabularies, and at the same time to clarify the meaning.

8. Encourage students to talk freely and listen carefully.

LAW #4—THE LAW OF THE LESSON: *Truth that is taught must be learned through truth already known.*

This law deals directly with the lesson or truth to be taught, and it is fundamental to all learning. A teacher must begin with what is already well known to the pupil about the subject and with what the pupil has already experienced and proceed to the new material by single, easy, and natural steps, letting the known explain the unknown. All teaching must begin at this known point of contact. If the subject is entirely new, a teacher must seek to find a known point of contact with students.

Jesus was a master of this law. He constantly built new truths on well-known facts. Since His learners were familiar with the Old Testament, He constantly explained New Testament events and concepts in terms of the Old. His crucifixion was similar to the lifting up of the brazen serpent in the wilderness. His burial and resurrection were likened to the story of Jonah in the belly of the whale. The times of His return would be like the days of Noah and Lot. For the most part, Jesus portrayed future events in terms of the past.

To observe this law, be aware of these related procedures.

1.   *Relate to former lessons.* You may assume that what has already been studied lies in the realm of the known. Making reference to former lessons is a good way to stay on familiar ground with your students. Every review is a demonstration of this law, and those who emphasize review best observe this principle.

2.   *Proceed by graded steps.* Athletes set their goal at a level they have not yet attained and then seek to attain it. Starting at a level that they can attain, they then advance little by little until they reach their goal and/or a new goal is established. In the same way, a student must fully grasp each truth before exploring and understanding the next one. New ideas become part of the student's knowledge and serve as a starting place for each fresh advance.

3.   *Illuminate by illustration.* When the advance of learning is too rapid for the mind to follow, making reference to known scenes permits the understanding to catch up. Figures of speech— such as similes, metaphors and allegories—have sprung out of the new lesson. Well-chosen stories connect new concepts to familiar settings.

4.   *Guide toward transfer of learning.* This law also applies to the transfer of what students have learned in one situation to another. If the known situation and the unknown are similar and have enough elements in common, learners may be able to transfer their responsibility to help students see the common elements and the broader application of biblical principles.

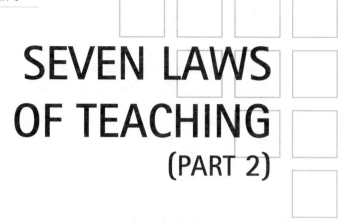

CHAPTER 6

SEVEN LAWS
OF TEACHING
(PART 2)

LAW #5—THE LAW OF THE TEACHING PROCESS: *The teacher must motivate and direct the self-activities of the learners.*

It is not enough for students to learn Bible facts; they must begin to live Bible truths. Your job is not complete until you arouse interest on the part of your students and help them begin to make the Bible teaching a part of their own lives. To accomplish this, you must deal with students as individuals, leading them to think for themselves. The learning process is accelerated when students become independent investigators. Yet teachers are necessary elements in the process as well. Among other things, good teachers provide favorable conditions for self-learning. They do not merely impart knowledge but stimulate their students to acquire it. They motivate their students and make available the resources students need in order to do independent study.

Teachers wishing to help students to become self-learners must:

1. *Provide thoughtful material.* Mental processes are limited to the field of acquired knowledge. Students who lack knowledge cannot think, for they have nothing to think about. In order to compare, criticize, judge, and reason, the mind must work on the materials in its own possession. For this reason, students need factual information that will serve as the basis of thought. Although it is true that education is in part a drawing-out process (teachers seeking to "draw out" knowledge from within students), teachers cannot draw out knowledge that has not been previously implanted.

2.   *Provoke investigation.* It is important to arouse the spirit of investigation. Rich educational processes begin when students ask who, what, when, where, why, and how. The maturing mind grapples with the problems of the universe. The falling apple caused the inquiring mind of Newton to ask the question about gravity. The boiling teakettle caused Watt to ask questions that led to the invention of the steam engine. The question is an index both to the students' minds and to their inner lives. Questions lead to self-realization and self-seeking. You should stimulate this natural quest for knowledge, as well as a natural desire for expression.

3.   *Provide satisfaction.* When students derive pleasure from what they are doing, they are more likely to continue the activity. This is known as reward or reinforcement. The tendency is to repeat those experiences that are satisfying and avoid those which are not. Satisfaction will be provided where learning is helpful to students' daily lives and where it meets their needs. You have the opportunity to make the learning experience worthwhile for your students.

LAW #6—THE LAW OF THE LEARNING PROCESS: *The student must integrate into his or her own life the truth that has been taught.*

Effective teachers arouse and guide the self-activities of their students and evaluate their students' responses. They help students to evaluate new truths and translate them into the art and skill of basic daily living. Despite these efforts, it is students who must decide to become learners if real education is to take place. Learning requires active interest, attention, and a clear and distinct act or process that only students can perform. They must cultivate their own minds by their own powers to achieve a true concept of the facts or principles of the lesson.

The work of education is more the work of students than of the teachers. True learning is more than repetition or regurgitation of lifeless data. Original discovery is a thrilling, stimulating process. The discoverer borrows facts known to others and adds that which he or she has learned by experience. Teachers use this law to guide students to be independent investigators.

There are at least three distinct stages of learning: reproduction, interpretation, and application. These are similar to the steps of learning in the first two chapters.

1. *Reproduction.* It is possible to reproduce the exact words of any lesson by committing them to memory. However, students who do not understand what they have memorized do not truly possess the lesson. Real learning requires that students be able to express the content of the lesson in their own words and in terms of their own experiences.

2. *Interpretation.* When students are able to advance beyond the memorization of facts, they give evidence that learning has taken place. Likewise, when they are able to express their own opinion of these facts, they understand what they have learned. They are able to deal with their own thoughts as well as the thoughts of others. Failure to insist on original thinking is a common fault of untrained teachers. Good teachers go beyond asking questions that can be answered with factual information alone. Instead, they ask "why" so the students learn to think for themselves.

3. *Application.* No lesson is fully learned until it is applied to life. Knowledge is power—but only when it is conquered, harnessed, and put to work. Expressing an opinion may exercise the mind, but applying knowledge affects the will and transforms the life of the learner. If practical, personal application is neglected, students will be "always learning and never able to acknowledge the truth" (2 Tim. 3:7). This is mere "head knowledge" and does not result in the life changing, transforming operation of God's grace.

LAW #7—THE LAW OF REVIEW AND APPLICATION: *The teacher and student must continually review and apply the truth taught.*

Business sessions often open with the reading of the minutes of the previous meeting and close with a report of the current day's proceedings. These exercises are reviews of what transpired at the beginning and end of the meeting. The first review establishes a close relationship with former sessions. The second carries the day's proceedings into the next meeting. In the same way, it is important in teaching to make contact with former lessons at the beginning of each lesson. It is equally essential that each lesson be carried over to the next lesson and that all learning be vitalized in the lives of the students. Review reinforces previous learning and deepens its impression by linking it with new ideas.

This law involves a practice of three areas of emphasis.

1. *Strengthen and perfect knowledge.* Although repetition is often involved in the process, review is more than repetition. It is an attempt to refocus facts and principles. It also provides the opportunity to gain deeper insight and to tie previous knowledge to new situations. So it is with Bible study. No other book needs more careful study or is so filled with treasures and blessings.

2. *Remember and confirm knowledge.* A person who is introduced to a group of people once may not remember many of the names. Later, when he sees and talks with a member of this group, however, he will review the names and his memory will be strengthened. The lesson that is studied only once will soon be forgotten. What is repeatedly reviewed will be permanently remembered and used.

3. *Apply and practice knowledge.* Frequent and thorough review renders knowledge readily useful. The Scripture texts that help us most are those that we have applied and used. Truths that have become familiar by repetition can shape conduct and mold character. The "line upon line and precept upon precept" rule of the Bible is recognition of this truth.

LET'S GET PRACTICAL

Effective teaching is both an art and a science. As an art, there is a certain unpredictability and fluidity to the process. As a science, it is governed by discernible laws of teaching and learning. Both of these aspects are amply illustrated in the teaching ministry of Jesus.

As a teacher, you must know your subject material, speak in a language students can understand, and introduce new ideas in terms of what students already know.

The act of learning itself, however, is done by students. No learning can be accomplished unless their interest and attention are maintained. Students must be led to desire to learn the truth that is presented. As they think ideas into their own understanding and develop new behavioral patterns, genuine learning takes place. Ultimately, the test of teaching success or failure is what happens in the lives of students.

FOR FURTHER DISCUSSION

1. What are some practical ways to motivate your students?

2. Why is student satisfaction important in learning?

3. How would you utilize each law of teaching in a future lesson?

SELECT BIBLIOGRAPHY

John Milton Gregory, *The Laws of Teaching* (Grand Rapids: Baker, 1954, 1975).

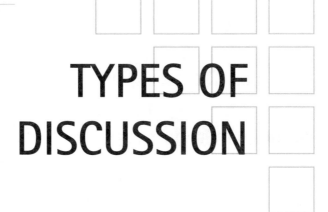

CHAPTER 7

TYPES OF DISCUSSION

THE DISCUSSION method occurs when the teacher stimulates the thinking of the student with carefully worded questions that prompt the student to examine in his or her own mind the issues presented in the lesson. The teacher then allows the student to respond to those questions and make contributions while carefully guiding the discussion to arrive at valuable conclusions.

THE VALUE OF THE DISCUSSION METHOD

Why use the discussion method when many are satisfied with using the tried and true lecture method of teaching? Although there are many values to this method, we will mention three basic ones:

(1) Using this method makes the student feel he is making a valuable contribution to the lesson presentation. He or she is not just a spectator, sitting on the sidelines and watching the action. The student participates in the action and contributes thinking to the process.

(2) Using this method encourages the student to make personal and practical application of the lesson text based on life experiences. No longer can the student be neutral about the claims of the lesson. The student must see within himself or herself those areas that need changing, and decide what is necessary to bring about that change.

(3) Using this method is beneficial for the teacher because it reveals the real concerns of the student's and the student's discussions contribute to the lesson and actually reveals to all what is on his or her mind. Sometimes this can be the very key to unlocking the understanding of the teacher as to how to get across to the student in future class periods.

CAUTIONS TO BE OBSERVED

Although this is an effective method of teaching the lesson, to obtain the desired results there are some precautions that must be observed by the teacher.

(1) Do not think that using the discussion method is a substitute for adequate reparation. What some call discussion is not discussion at all, but just a gathering of various opinions from those who have never studied the lesson. The effective use of this method will require even more preparation than usual because the teacher will have to be prepared for any eventuality.

(2) Never allow the session to become negative in tone. Some will try to use the discussion to "air" their gripes before the rest of the class, or raise their favorite confusing criticism. Do not rebuke such attempts openly, but do move on to a more constructive area quickly.

(3) Avoid side issues that are not relevant to the question under consideration. It is very easy to leave the main trail of the discussion and "run rabbit trails" because of the diverse make-up of the class. The wise teacher will meticulously avoid this temptation so that the maximum good can be accomplished in the time allowed for discussion.

(4) Never lose control of the discussion. The teacher must always be in control moderating all that is considered. Some in the class will unconsciously attempt to take over the lead, but the teacher must kindly take control and keep it throughout the discussion. This is the only way that the discussion can be kept on track.

TYPES OF DISCUSSION

In our attempts to be as practical as possible, we will mention only those types of discussion sessions that could be effectively used in the average Sunday School class or small groups.

(1) **SMALL GROUP DISCUSSION.** I am devoting a whole chapter on this type of discussion because of how effective it can be. After stating the question or topic to be considered, divide the class into groups. The total number in the class will determine how many groups of three to five. Have each group come up with possible solutions to the question or contributions relative to the topic. Set a time limit on their sessions together. Then have them assemble as a class after the time is up to make their contributions. Have each group appoint a spokesman to report on what the group has decided about the question. After receiving the comments from the leaders of each group, than ask for general responses.

(2) **READ AND REPORT.** Ahead of time, assign several topics that concern the lesson to choice student in the class. Give them the responsibility of reporting their findings back to the class. This may be a practical problem that all are concerned about, the gathering of the opinions of the church about a practical consideration in the lesson, or a technical matter involving Biblical interpretation. By having the student research ahead of time and report back to the class, the student will have learned much more from the lesson. This contribution will enlighten others as well.

(3) **REQUESTED RESPONSES.** In the lesson presentation itself, the teacher may request the students to respond on any number of matters as they arise. For instance, the teacher may ask someone to read aloud some important verse, then call for the observations of the class members about the important points contained in the verse. The class may be asked to comment on their opinion about the practical application of a verse of Scripture, and asked to list those applications on the marker board for everyone else to see. In each case, the teacher is responsible for calling for the responses and deciding which would be included in the list and which would be rejected.

(5) **PANEL DISCUSSION.** Divide the lesson up into three or four parts, assigning a part to one student to do extra work and study on, and set a time when the ones assigned the extra study can report as a panel on what they have learned. Assign a time limit to stay in for reporting so then one will not dominate too much time in the lesson. After they have reported on their findings, the class can then ask them questions about their report, or discuss more fully what they have presented.

(6) **CIRCUMSTANTIAL DIALOGUE.** There are times when things happen in the community that require a special time in the classroom. If some tragic event has occurred, a catastrophe, or an accident that has shocked the people in the nation or community, there should be some sort of dialogue encouraged among the students. They will want to talk about it, and the wise teacher will direct their thoughts along the lines of the teaching of Scripture and how to apply the Scriptures to their grief, anger, or other emotions. On such occasions the regular order of the class will be suspended in favor of allowing this outpouring of frustration. This kind of discussion will be healing in its effect, as well as instructional for the future when these things may occur again. For effective use of the circumstantial dialogue this cannot occur frequently and once again the teacher must adequately prepare to help biblically guide the discussion.

HOW TO CONDUCT A LIVELY DISCUSSION SESSION

This pattern is not meant to be an absolute for everyone, but just a way of showing the inexperienced how to begin using this valuable method of teaching the Word.

1. Choose your subject. Do not allow the subject of the discussion to just "come up" in the course of the lesson. Plan what you are going to throw out for response from the students. Choose the subject well, for your choice will determine the interest and response of the students.

2. Write out a list of questions. Avoid questions that can be answered with a simple "yes" or "no." Make the questions demand a response from the student. Questions that begin with "How do you feel about . . . "; "When do you think . . . "; "Is there any reason . . . "; etc., are good thought provokers. By writing the questions out, you will have a continuous source of questions to ask should one question not create any response on the part of the students.

3. Be prepared! Do not make the mistake of thinking that the student will teach the lesson for you. In fact, the teacher will have to be more adequately prepared than usual for this kind of teaching, for there is no way of knowing what the student will bring up in the course of the discussion.

4. After asking the question, be quiet. Allow silence to prompt someone to answer. If you have never taught using discussion you may experience a long silence at the first couple of questions asked. Do not feel obligated to answer your question yourself. Let your students do so. It will then cause them to know you want their input and are not just asking rhetorical questions.

5. Throw the question out for general response in order to see who is on the wave length of the teacher. Sometimes this may be surprising as the students pick up on the question immediately and begin to express themselves in an animated manner.

6. Ask for specific response from particular people if the discussion bogs down and moves slowly. Be sure that you ask those who would not be embarrassed by such exposure or questions. Never embarrass a guest by calling on them. Let them speak out during general response.

7. Carry the discussion by referring progressive comments to each of the students, or picking up on what one has said and applying it to the question at hand. Be complimentary to the students as they speak and thus encourage others to comment as well. "That's a good suggestion . . . "; "Can anyone help Beth with this . . . "; or "Ethan has made an excellent observation . . . " are all comments which will make the next student respond.

8. Arrive at definite conclusions. Do not allow the discussion to be open-ended, that is, to drift along without coming to some conclusion about the original question. Have the students contribute what they think ought to be done with this question, and write their contributions on the marker board. If it is a practical matter, encourage them to put the suggestions into practice.

A FINAL WORD

Do not be afraid to try this exciting method of teaching in your class. Variety is the spice of life, and variety in teaching methods is the spark that will hold the interest of your students causing them to make personal applications of the lesson to their lives.

CHAPTER 8

SMALL GROUP DISCUSSION

NEXT WE will discuss the method known as small group discussion. A small group discussion happens when you divide the entire class into two or more smaller groups, with two to five members in each small group. As the small group meets for a limited time, they discuss a topic that the teacher has suggested and then report back to the class on their discoveries. The following diagrams compare the lecture method with the small group discussion method:

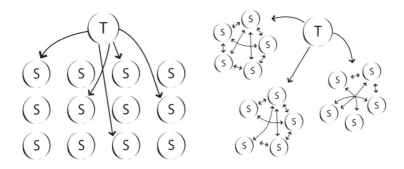

The small group discussion does not replace the lecture method but small groups discussions are used to assist the teacher in making the lecture more meaningful to the class.

PURPOSES

The purposes of the small group will vary as much as the subject matter.

1)   To discuss or study quickly a topic or topics of interest.

2)   To involve the entire class in discussion and study.

3)   To promote interaction and fellowship within the class.

4)   To provide a variety of methodology.

5)   To keep the attention and interest of the class at a high level.

6)   To multiply the efforts of the class so that everyone receives the knowledge gained in each group.

7)   To help class members better know fellow classmates.

TIME

For most situations in your small group or Sunday School class giving five to ten minutes are adequate for most topics. An interesting way to watch the time is for the teacher to use an egg kitchen timer to time the period predetermined for the small group. The teacher sets the time limit and when time is up, the bell goes off. If one is unavailable, the teacher can call or announce when time is half way along and then announce a two minutes warning, one minute and then thirty seconds to summarize. Remember in planning that it will take at least a couple of minutes or so for the class to move their chairs into the smaller groups and back again.

Also, one small group session per lesson is usually more than adequate. Some classes will want to use this method more and other classes less. You, as the teacher, will need to use your judgment in deciding the frequency of use.

ASSIGNMENTS

The teacher has the responsibility to make the assignments that control the activities of the small groups. These assignments fall into two areas.

1. **TOPIC**

   The topic assignments are obviously dependent on the subject matter in the passage you are studying. You may desire for each small group to tackle a different question or subject, or you may desire for each group to discuss the same question or subject.

   Examples of the above types of small groups can be found in most curriculum publisher's material.

2. **GROUP MAKE-UP**

   Not only will you wish to assign topics to the groups, but you may wish to assign particular people to certain groups. Since one of the purposes of small groups is to help your people get acquainted, be sure to select people to be in groups that do not normally sit together.

   A simple way of accomplishing this is to have the class number themselves by say "1 . . . 2 . . . 3 . . . 4" depending on the number of groups you wish to have. After everyone has a number have all the ones group together and all twos and so forth. Explain what you want each group to accomplish and then set aside places in the room for the groups to meet. As the teacher, you may appoint someone to be the leader of the group or permit each group to choose its own.

SEATING

Depending on the physical make-up of your room, you will either want the students to change location or to "take up their chairs and walk." If your classroom has pews, you will be forced to move people. If your classroom has movable chairs, move the chairs. Either way, some type of circle or semicircle approach seems best. Care should be taken that time is not wasted or that noise is too great a factor.

TEACHER'S ROLE

The teacher not only has the responsibility of selecting the topic and dividing the class but also of overseeing the work of each small group. This is especially important if this is a new method for your class, and they are uncertain as to exactly what they are supposed to be doing.

During the actual small group time, you should walk around among the groups to answer any questions and to encourage everyone's participation in the activity. You can serve best by complimenting good answers resulting in promoting participation as well as affirming they are "on topic." It is best that you *not* be involved as a member of a group but stay free as a resource person for any group that needs help.

WRAP-UP

When the time you have set aside for the small group is up, ask the students to turn their attention to you. Some teachers may wish to allow everyone to go back to their original seats before the group discussion. Others may wish to wait until the group discussion has been completed.

Basically, this wrap-up is time given to the groups for the reports of what was discovered in each small group. Care must be taken not to spend too much time in simply repeating what has already been said. It is often helpful to write a summary of each group's findings on the marker board for all the class to see. This will also assist you in concluding the particular exercise and keep others from repeating what has already been said.

As the reports are being made, you should quietly think of some major conclusions that can be drawn from what has been learned. In many cases, you will have already thought these conclusions through in your own personal study of the lesson. You may wish to list these conclusions on the board as the end of the reports or encourage the class to verbalize the conclusions they have drawn in their own minds. Be sure that there is a point to your use of small group. Make the application practical and plain.

CONCLUSION

If you have never used small groups in your teaching before, start out slowly. You will discover that some adults will love the buzz group method; other adults will dislike it and prefer the lecture method. You know your class best, so use your own judgment in deciding if this method will be successful in your class.

Only use one small group activity in each lesson. You will find that small groups discussions consume a lot of time if they are not controlled. They should *never* be used as time fillers or "discuss anything your want" times. Be sure that you let the class know exactly what each group is to do and how much time they have to do it in. Then stick to your timetable!

After using the small group discussion method, ask the members of the class what they thought of it and what they would suggest to make it better. Listen to what your students are really saying about your teaching methods and make the proper adjustments.

Small group discussion can be a very meaningful addition to your teaching ministry methodology. Give small group discussion an opportunity to be a blessing to your class!

CHAPTER 9

CASE STUDIES

WHAT IS A CASE STUDY?

ACCORDING TO LEROY FORD, author of *Using the Case Study in Teaching and Training* (Broadman Press), the case study is "an account of a problem situation including enough detail for learners to suggest possible solutions." In essence, the case study is simply a story with which the members of the class can get involved. Thus, the case study is more than story telling, it is problem-solving.

An example of a case study would be:

There was an old woman who
   lived in a shoe
She had so many children she
   didn't know what to do.
She gave them some broth, without
   any bread,
And whipped them all soundly,
   and sent them to bed.

Several questions arise from this story.

1.   Is this woman married? Is she a widow? Is she divorced?

2.   Where in the world did she get a shoe big enough to live in?

3. Why isn't she on welfare?

4. Is she guilty of child abuse?

5. What can the church do to help her situation?

6. If she came to you for help, what would you do?

The main point of this case study is to get the class to think of ways that this old woman, if she really existed, could be helped. Of course, the case studies you use should be much more realistic than a nursery rhyme. (Although, if you put this woman in an apartment in the inner city, it could be very realistic!) The point is use the case study to present a problem, and then lead your class in a discussion of how to solve it.

WHY SHOULD I USE THE CASE STUDY?

There are several reasons why you should use the case study and how it will be profitable to your class.

1. The case study will help your class develop skills in making decisions by presenting a practice session for decision-making. The case study forces a person to decide in his or her own mind the best course of action in a particular situation.

2. The case study helps students to work with other class members in pooling their various resources and collective insights. It is possible in many situations that a classmate may express a viewpoint that you alone would have never considered.

3. The case study will help your students focus on concrete solutions to realistic problems. It will help them relate the "this I believe" of Christianity to the "this I do" of Christianity.

4. The case study helps the student to bridge the gap between theory and practice. Often, Sunday School or small groups deal only with Bible content and time is not spent in relating that Bible content to everyday, real life situations. The case study forces the students to apply Biblical principles to all of life.

5.   The case study can help the students to see their own problems in perspective. Often, a good case study may parallel a problem or situation in the life of a class member. This will not only help the student see that he or she is not alone in this problem, but gains the insight of the class in helping to solve the problem.

6.   The case study helps to increase involvement in the teaching-learning process. The individual members of the class must get involved. The case study is designed to be a group activity.

7.   The case study will train the members of your class to think better independently as well as collectively.

These seven reasons (there are many others) declare that the case study can help your students to see their own problems more clearly, to think better individually and as a group, and to creatively apply Biblical teachings to everyday life. Case studies really help students assimilate the material taught.

WHERE DO I FIND CASE STUDIES?

1.   Newspapers and news magazines. Be ready to clip an interesting tidbit, situation, or biographical sketch.

2.   The Internet provides a plethora of material, social sites of people with problems to news sources and even videos if you can play them in class.

3.   Advice columns, such as "Dear Abby" and "Ann Landers." Clip out interesting questions and have the class come up with their own Biblical solution to the problem.

4.   Christian magazines will contain lots of usable information of all kinds that can easily be related to most any Bible lesson.

5.   Believe it or not, cartoon and comic strips can often be used as case studies. Many times, comic strips such as *Peanuts* give insight into real-life problems and situations in a comical way. You can use single-frame cartoons without the caption and have the class fill it in as a change of pace.

6. Biographies of great Christian men and women contain much material suitable for use as a case study.

PRACTICAL POINTS ON CASE STUDIES

Here are some practical insights for how to use case studies in your small group or Sunday School class.

1. Do not overuse the case study or it well lose some of its effectiveness. One case study every other lesson or once a month is a good way to start out.

2. Encourage everyone to get involved in the case study. A simple outline to use is:

   a. Define the problem.

   b. Get the facts and fit them together.

   c. Determine several possible solutions and their results.

   d. Choose the best solution.

3. Have enough facts in the case study to keep the class discussion on target. The responsibility of the teacher is to be sure that the class stays on the subject at hand based on the material being taught.

4. Always lead the class to a definite conclusion with a case study if at all possible. Help them to decide on one solution or several possible solutions to the case study.

Above all, determine to use the case study at least once in the coming month. You may find that it will open doors of in-depth thought and student involvement that will lead to practical application of Biblical truth.

CHAPTER 10

STORYTELLING

IMAGINE YOU ARE TEACHING a young teens' Sunday School class and the lesson focuses on the deceptive nature of sin. The Bible text is Galatians 6:7, which says, "Do not be deceived: God cannot be mocked. A man reaps what he sows." To introduce this lesson, you tell your class the following true story.

Grant Williams, 19 years old, shared his Bronx, New York apartment with his younger brother Lamar and their, 85-pound 13-foot, five-inch thick beige and brown Burmese python. The snake, purchased at a local pet shop for $300, lived in a cage in their apartment. The brothers frequently took the snake out of its cage to show it off to friends in the neighborhood. The brothers fed the snake live chickens. But one afternoon, after Grant had taken the python out of its cage, something went horribly wrong. A few minutes later, a neighbor found Grant lying in the doorway of his apartment with the python wrapped tightly around his throat. Paramedics were called. Upon arrival they struggled to pry the snake off of Grant's body. But it was too late. He was pronounced dead an hour later at a local hospital.

Local authorities investigated the incident and determined the python had mistaken its owner for its meal because it could smell a chicken on the young man's hands: a chicken he had bought earlier that day to feed to his pet. Grant's heartbroken brother later told reporters, "The snake was trained. We trusted that snake. I never thought it would hurt any of us."

What a tragedy! These young men trusted their pet snake, but unfortunately, a snake can only be trusted to do what its nature compels it to do. Thus, these men were sadly deceived. They trusted in the wrong thing. In our Bible lesson today, God is warning us not to be deceived by listening to voices other than His own.1

Would this story capture the attention of a young teen? Did it capture yours? Do you believe the students would be more motivated or less motivated to become involved in the rest of the lesson after hearing this story? Finally, do you think these students would remember this story and the point it was trying to make?

Stories are powerful teaching tools. Whether we are young or old, stories that are well-told and properly used command our attention, stimulate our imagination, focus our spirit on a particular moral or ethical dilemma, and can put us emotionally "inside the skin" of another person. Stories can help us see ourselves and others more clearly and with greater empathy than we would otherwise. Stories can help make propositional truth come alive and connect Biblical principles with real life.

Max McLean is president of the Fellowship for the Performing Arts and tours the country presenting books of the Bible as one-man theatrical productions. McLean has written:

A story is merely a conversation between a narrator and his audience. But a good story well told is a reminder of the priceless worth of that exchange. If a story is told well enough you will follow it anywhere—even if it leads to places you never expected to go. At first, its familiarity appears like a well-worn path. Then a moment arrives . . . when you realize that you have strayed into an area that scrapes against the edge of the soul. There is a slight chill, evoking something akin to goose bumps, but with a thrilling warmth that attends those rare moments of unforeseen insight.[2]

All great teachers are great storytellers. To become a master teacher, you must master the art and technique of storytelling.

WHY USE STORYTELLING?

Why should a teacher use the method of storytelling?

1. *The Bible itself is one big story—the story of redemption.* One cannot read the Bible without encountering stories. Every type of story exists in Scripture. There are tragedies, comedies, love stories and adventure tales. There are Bible stories about men and women, children and teenagers, heroes and villains, kings and slaves, acts of bravery and acts of treachery. All of the stories of the Bible, however, have one thing in common: they are recorded so we can more clearly understand the "big" story the Bible is telling. In similar fashion, teachers should tell "little" stories that help to illuminate the "big" story. The main storyline of the Bible is God's love for humankind expressed through the death, burial, and resurrection of His Son, Jesus Christ. Every one of the 66 books of the Bible is centered on this storyline. The stories teachers tell should always point to God's big story. Since God has used stories to communicate with us, we should also use stories to communicate with our students.

2. *The Old Testament contains numerous examples of storytelling.* In fact, much of the Old Testament is written in story form. How many Old Testament stories can you easily recount? The entire Old Testament is the story of how God created a race of people, watched the race rebel against Him, called a man to follow Him, and from that man made a nation from which a Redeemer would come. For specific Old Testament examples of the use of stories in a teaching situation, see Judges 9:7-20; 2 Samuel 12:1-13; the entire books of Esther and Job; and Ezekiel 17: 1-15.

3. *Storytelling was the major methodology used by Jesus.* Careful analysis of the teaching methods of Jesus will reveal He was a master storyteller. Often, Jesus' stories are referred to as parables. The word "parable" means to "throw along side of." Thus, the idea is that parable is a story that parallels one or more propositional truths being taught. [3] Many teachers learned that

"a parable is an earthly story with a heavenly meaning," and this is true. But parable-telling is not limited to those Jesus told. A parable is simply any story, true or made-up, that illustrates a spiritual truth. The key to Jesus' use of stories is that He knew His audience intimately and was therefore able to use settings, characters, and plot lines familiar to His audience.

4. *Stories capture the attention and imagination of your students.* Just as the snake story at the beginning of this chapter was one that "hooked" you into reading further, so stories can be effectively used to introduce Bible lessons. Stories also have the unique ability to paint mental images and to produce an emotional reaction. It is possible to ignore propositional truth no matter how well it is presented, but it is very difficult to reject a story without first interacting with it. This is just the way God has created us.

5. *Stories can be custom-designed for our students.* Master teachers who are great storytellers not only know how to tell stories but they know how to select (or write) stories that appeal to their students because they know their students' needs, hopes, and fears. Wise teachers can literally "tailor-make" stories for their students.

6. *Storytelling can easily be used with other methodologies.* One of the dangers for teachers who like to use storytelling is they may neglect other methods. Any method improperly utilized or overused will result in poor teaching. However, storytelling used to balance with other methodologies can take your teaching to the next level.

7. *Stories help to connect Bible truths to modern day situations.* Someone has said the process of teaching the Bible is one that starts where we are, takes us to the lands of the Bible (through the Scriptures), and then back home again. All three steps are important, and effective storytelling skills can be useful at all three steps in the process. A story from current events can stimulate our students to think about the topic to be studied and can easily lead into the Bible passage. A well-told story about biblical characters can make them come alive, help stu-

dents to see the similarities between their times and our own, and lead the students to apply the Bible to their lives.

8. *Stories are long remembered.* Think about all the Bible lessons and sermons you have heard in your own life. What do you remember? Is it the title? The outline? The gestures? For most of us, the stories are what we remember. Why? As suggested above, God has created us this way. A well-chosen, properly told story can be used by the Holy Spirit to change lives and will often remain stored in our memories.

BASIC COMPONENTS OF A STORY

All stories share the following elements:

A setting—Where and when does the story take place? A setting can be vague ("long ago in a faraway place"), specific ("it was October 10, 1984 and the streets of Las Vegas were strangely quiet"), or assumed ("a certain man was going down to Jericho"). For some students, the more details you share about the setting, the more alive it will become. For others, fewer details provide a greater opportunity for their imaginations to fit the setting into their own context.

Characters—Who is involved in the story? Every story has at least one character, but most stories have two or more. In telling stories to illustrate teaching points, limit the characters. If you use too many characters in a short story, no one will remember any of them.

Plot—What happens in the story? Plot is simply the course of events happening to the character or characters. More involved stories may have one or more subplots. When telling stories in a teaching context, make sure the main plot remains the main plot.

Conflict—Upon what does the story hinge? What motivates the actions and reactions of the characters? For example, in the story of Joseph, all the action hinges on the conflict between Joseph and his brothers; in the story of Daniel and the lion's den, there is a conflict between Daniel and the other governmental officials. Although in some stories, the conflict is an internal one, all stories have a conflict of some kind. "Matt wore a brown shirt" is not a story, but "Matt decided to wear a brown shirt even though his teacher told him never to do so" is at least the beginning of a story. Why? Because there is a conflict.

Resolution—How does the story end? As Paul Harvey, one of the most famous American radio broadcasters to live, liked to say, "That's the rest of the story." Good storytellers do not "tip their hand" by giving away the resolution of the story too soon. People do not like unresolved conflict. Thus, your students will keep listening to your story to learn how events will turn out.

Moral—What is the main point of the story? Often the moral of a well-told story will be obvious. Sometimes, the storyteller may wish to state it clearly so there can be no misunderstanding of why the story was told. Still other times, the teacher may present the question of moral to the class by asking students the meaning of the story. If you use this last technique, do not be surprised to discover that more than one meaning has been derived from the same story. This is one of the powers of stories.

Voice—How is the story told? A story may be told in the first person, or in other words, a story that has happened to you personally. This technique, however, is not limited to stories you have actually experienced. For example, it can be very effective to dress up like a Biblical character and then tell the story in the character's own words. Most stories are told in the third person from the perspective of a narrator who knows the actions, and often the thoughts of the characters.

PRINCIPLES OF STORYTELLING

Here are some basic pointers on how to become a good storyteller.

1. *If at all possible, do not read the story.* You may need to read a story out loud a few times to get the basics of it in your memory, but a story told is infinitely more powerful than a story read.

2. *Practice, practice, practice.* Storytelling is a skill to be developed. Practice telling stories at home, to your friends, and in work and social contexts. If you own any type of voice recorder or a video camera, practice telling a story and then critique yourself.

3. *Be an ethical storyteller.*

- *Give credit when possible.* If you first heard Dr. Tony Evans or Dr. John Maxwell tell the story, tell your students. The power of a story is not diluted because you acknowledge your source.

- *Ask permission to use someone else's story told to you in private.* Do not share stories about other family members without their permission. Do not tell stories to manipulate people's emotions or to produce a false guilt. This is especially important to remember in teaching children.

- *Do not say a story is true unless you are sure it is.* It is always permissible to make up a story as long as you do not say or imply it really happened. You can always say, "The story is told . . . " or "I don't know whether this story is true or not . . . ."

- *Do not tell a story like it happened to you if it did not.* As I said above, the power of a story is not diluted because it happened to someone else. However, if you tell a story as if it really happened to you and it did not, it can severely damage your credibility.

- *Use autobiographical references cautiously.* When you do share personal stories, do not make yourself the star/hero of every story you tell. Be careful not to embarrass other members of your family.

- *Use humor carefully.* A story does not have to be funny to be remembered. However, a humorous story poorly told or one that uses off-color content will be remembered, but for all the wrong reasons.

4. *Do not be afraid of allowing your students to draw their own conclusions from a story.* Especially with youth and adults, you do not always have to spell out the "moral of the story." If it is a good story and fits well with the Bible text, the moral should be obvious. Allow your students to make connections for themselves.

5. *Tell stories with appropriate use of tone and gestures.* The two best

audio-visual aids are your voice and your body. The change in volume and pitch of your voice will sustain interest in the story. A well-timed pause will also help to focus student attention. Do not be afraid to use your hands and arms in storytelling.

Other helps can assist you in storytelling. For children, pictures and posters can give them an image and setting of what you are teaching. Many churches have files of posters with Bible story scenes. These posters, when properly used, can also add to the storytelling experience. For teens and adults, multimedia such as a clip from a DVD or PowerPoint. Keep in mind, however, the best audio-visual aids cannot make up for an improperly chosen or poorly told story.

6. *Listen carefully to other storytellers and analyze their technique.* Pay attention to the stories you hear every day from family members, friends, co-workers, teachers, workshop leaders, and performers on radio or television. What aspect of the story or storytelling technique captured your attention? What techniques of storytelling can you learn from this person? What techniques were incorrectly used?

CRITERIA FOR CHOOSING STORIES

Equally important to the mastery of storytelling technique is the mastery of proper story selection.

1. *Select stories to fit the Scripture you are teaching, not the other way around.* It is better not to tell a story and to use another method in its place than to use a story that does not fit well with the Bible passage. If you want to use a story to illustrate a point of your lesson but are at a loss for finding one, consider whether there are any Bible stories that fit the criteria.

2. *Select stories to meet the needs of your students.* Effective storytellers know their students! The age and life situation of your students will affect the storytelling choices you make.

3. *Select stories that achieve the desired goal of your teaching point.* The three major types of teaching goals are informational, in-

spirational/motivational, and volitional (moving to action).

SOURCES OF STORIES

Stories can be found by utilizing the following sources.

1. *Bible stories*—Both Old and New Testaments are filled with stories that illustrate every conceivable truth. In this way, we can literally "interpret Scripture by Scripture."

2. *Historical events*—Stories from history, whether it be ancient, medieval, or modern, world or American, are easily found in libraries, encyclopedias, or on the Internet.

3. *Stories from fiction*—The great stories from the world of fiction, such as those from Grimm's fairy tales, Charles Dickens, Ernest Hemingway, and C. S. Lewis, can be effectively used in Bible teachings.

4. *Television, movies, and Internet*—We are living in a digital world. Today's high school and college students are technology saturated. Illustrations from these mediums will connect with them.

5. *Current events found in newspapers and magazines*—Teachers should read at least one newspaper a day and browse through popular news magazines on a regular basis. Even if you cannot afford your own subscription, public libraries have these items available for free.

6. *Made-up stories*—If you cannot find an appropriate story to fit your Bible lesson, write it yourself. As long as you do not try to pass it off as a true story, this can be very effective. You can start such a story by saying, "Imagine if . . . or "I would like to share with you the parable of the . . ." or even "The story is told. . ."

7. *Personal anecdotes*—Stories of events that have actually happened to you can be very effective. Often, these are the easiest to tell. However, care must be taken not to embellish them or overuse them.

8. *Illustration books*—There are many books available containing compilations of stories that can be very helpful in finding just

the right story.

9. *Illustration software programs*—Similar to illustration books, a number of companies have produced such resources as CD-ROM which allow for fast searching by topic, word, or Bible passage.

10. *Illustration services*—Illustration services offer contemporary stories on a regular basis to subscribers.

11. *The Internet*—There are numerous illustration resources available on the Internet, many of them at no charge. At press time, one website provided links to over 50 sites which provide free illustrations as well as detailed descriptions for each.[4]

12. *Your own illustration files*—Be sure to faithfully file your story ideas. You will need to choose a system that works best for you, either organizing data by topic, by key word, or by Scripture passage. You may wish to cross-reference your stories. If you have a personal computer, you can use a simple database program to help organize your materials.

LET'S GET PRACTICAL

Storytelling is an important methodology and should be included in every teacher's toolbox of techniques. Ethel Barrett, in her classic *Storytelling—It's Easy,* wrote there are three essentials to the success of a story: the storyteller, the story, and the audience.[5] With proper attention to each of these three elements, you can become a teacher who is a successful storyteller.

TEACHING STUDENTS NOT LESSONS

ENDNOTES

[1]David Herszenhorn, "13-Foot-Long Pet Python Kills Its Caretaker." *New York Times* (October 10, 1996) and *JET* (November 4, 1996).

[2]Max McClean, "Program Notes for Genesis" (Morristown, NJ: Fellowship for the Performing Arts, 2000.)

[3]Matt Friedman, *The Master Plan of Teaching* (Wheaton: SP Publications, 1990), 168.

[4]See "Holwick's Links to the Best Free Sermon Illustrations" at *http://users.nac.net/whj2000/ill-link.html.*

[5]Ethel Barrett, *Storytelling – It's Easy* (Grand Rapids: Zondervan, 1960), 14.

CHAPTER 11

YOUNG ADULTS

YOUNG ADULTS COMPRISE around 20 percent of the American population according to recent statistics. The bulk of television and print advertising is aimed at this age group. As a whole, they are better educated than their parents and have often moved away from the area where they grew up. Most importantly, young adults are crucial to the growing church. Young adults are a valuable source of new converts, workers, teachers, children, and financial resources for the local church, not to mention passion, energy, and creativity.

In order to effectively minister to young adults, we must know something about them. Most older adults tend to base their understanding of young adulthood on their own experience as a young adult. Unfortunately, in today's changing society, the older adult's experience may have been vastly different from the crises that young adults face today.

DEFINITION OF THE TERM

The term *young adult* is a broad one and can include adults from the ages of 18 to 35, but more recently describes those 18-28. This describes those who are no longer in high school but are not entirely "settled." Young adults are simply those who are young at the business of being an adult. Age alone is no guarantee of maturity in an adult, neither is youth a sign of immaturity. Although the age range of young adulthood can be large, there are some common characteristics of young adults. Keep in mind there is no such thing as an "average" young adult but there are similar stages of life each young adult will pass through in one form or another.

YOUNG ADULT CHARACTERISTICS

A.   PHYSICAL AND SOCIAL DEVELOPMENT

1.   *Reaching their peak physically.* Young adults are as a whole healthy, energetic, and involved in varied forms of recreational activity. For example, professional athletes are in their prime during these years. Even young adults not involved in professional sports are highly conscious of their health, and many take significant strides to better it.

2.   *Adjusting to change internally and externally.* The young adult is faced with adjustments of every kind. Fortunately, most are better equipped to deal with the stresses of life than they were as teens. Moving away from home, dating, managing finances, marriage, their first child, all of these events demand adjustments of the young adult.

3.   *Establishing a personal identity apart from parents and peers.* Young adults are usually "on their own" and must find out something about who they are and where they are headed in life. Although parents and peers can help in this process, the ultimate answers must be found by the young adult.

4.   *Time of mobility.* Americans are a mobile people and young adults head the list as movers. Thus, the young adult must establish some roots in something other than home because most of them will end up far away from their original "roots."

5.   *Technology.* Young adults have been raised on technology. They are always connected to their friends and loved ones. This impacts how they work, play, and even worship.

6.   *Willing to engage.* Multi-cultural is the nation young adults grew up in. They are increasingly comfortable with coming into contact with many different people and faiths.

B.   EMOTIONAL AND INTELLECTUAL DEVELOPMENT

1.   *Stabilization of personal identity.* As young adults mature, they become more aware of who they are, their potential and some-

thing about God's plan. Their lifestyle during this time will establish patterns that will stick with them for a lifetime.

2. *Optimistic and idealistic.* Young adults are out to change their world, whether it is at school, at work, or at church. They have high ideals and expectations of the way things ought to be and are optimistic they can make a difference in the areas they are involved in. This spirit of optimism and idealism is often seen by older adults as a lack of respect for tradition and the "old paths." In truth, especially in the church, the young adult believes traditions that are not meeting real needs should be replaced with new traditions that meet spiritual needs and that tradition should be measured by the Bible, not man's opinions.

3. *Disillusioned and skeptic.* Young adults have been consistently disappointed. Their parents divorced. Their politicians lie. Their pastors had affairs. Everyone is trying to sell them something. As a result of these things, young adults are skeptic. They don't believe things just because someone claims it to be true. They will listen, though, and follow suit, if the truth is proven.

4. *Full intellectual capacity and ability to learn new things rapidly.* More and more young adults are continuing their education, going to technical schools, attending night courses, learning a new trade. The world demands intellectual development and young adults are accepting the challenge. Over two-thirds of all of Generation Y will receive a college degree, meaning more and more will receive graduate training as well.

C.   SPIRITUAL DEVELOPMENT

1. *Strengthening of their basic beliefs.* For young adults who have been believers for several years, there is a new hunger for the things of God and recommitment of their lives totally to Him. For the young adult who comes to know the Lord at this state of his life, there is an amazing eagerness to learn as much as possible about God and His Word. For the young adult who has been saved, there is a great desire to go back to the foundation in regard to why they believe what they do.

2. *A greater reliance on Scripture for personal guidance.* The Bible becomes real to the young adult. Passages and verses that seemed to be irrelevant are now important. The Word of God becomes the source of personal strength and the young adult is looking for a church that centers its ministry on the preaching and teaching of the Book in a real way that creates an experience of God.

3. *Evaluation of life goals and priorities.* Young adults are ripe for challenge to full-time Christian service. Many are going back to Bible colleges and seminaries to prepare for various ministries. Family life is seen as a top priority and many young adults need help in developing the best possible family life.

4. *A desire to be active in serving Christ.* Those who have chosen not to enter full-time service are looking for ways to be meaningfully involved in the local church. They are looking for opportunities that will be challenging and fulfilling. They want to serve their community. They want to make a tangible difference in the lives of the people around them.

5. *A need for fellowship with their peers.* Young adults need contact with adults their own age who share their commitment to Christ, His Word, and His church.

YOUNG ADULT LIFE TASKS

Young adults are facing a period of development in a variety of areas. All of these are ones that the church can help prepare them to face:

1. Understanding themselves,

2. Choice of career,

3. Establishing independence from parents,

4. Dealing with past hurts,

5. Marriage,

6. Decision to remain single,

7.   Children,

8.   Finding a church in which to be fed, fellowship, and serve.

YOUNG ADULT LIFE CRISES

The church needs to be aware of the crises that many young adults will face during this period of their lives. These crises cannot always be prepared for ahead of time but often must be adjusted to over a period of time. The church can help in these adjustments:

1.   Divorce (their own or their parents),

2.   Untimely death of spouse,

3.   Single parenthood,

4.   Dealing with homosexual desires,

5.   Death of a child/miscarriage,

6.   Birth of a handicapped child,

7.   Serious illness of spouse,

8.   Period of unemployment.

CONCLUSION

In order to minister effectively to young adults, whether it is in the small groups, Sunday School or any other church agency, there must be an understanding of who young adults are and the stages of development they are in and will be passing through. Obviously, this chapter is only a brief introduction to the subject.

Young adults are not teenagers. They are not middle or older adults. They are young adults and need to be understood as the people they are at the time of life they are experiencing. Will you accept the challenge to seek to better understand young adults in order to more effectively minister to their needs?

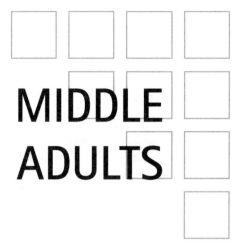

CHAPTER 12

MIDDLE ADULTS

THE YEARS FROM 28 TO 50 are commonly recognized as the period of "middle" or "median" adulthood. By far the longest period of the adult life cycle, these years are considered to be "prime time" in every area of life. Once this was the largest group in churches, "baby boomers," but they have grown past this category of ages. Recently the middle adult has been a shrinking age group in churches. In fact, the most noticeable group absent from church is the 18-30 year old category.

To minister effectively to the middle adult, one needs to get a good overview of the personality characteristics of the average middle adult. Keep in mind that while no "average middle adult" exists, there are several traits that most middle adults possess to a greater or lesser degree.

PHYSICAL AND SOCIAL CHARACTERISTICS

The middle adult years are the beginning of general physical decline. That is not to say that middle adults cannot be active or involved in strenuous physical work or exercise but rather that their bodies are not what they were in their twenties and early thirties. Thus, the teacher of middle adults should stress the importance of taking care of the body as the temple of God as well as the fact that what a person is on the inside is of much more value than the condition of the outside.

There is a change in work style for the middle adult from strength and quickness to wisdom and breadth of perspective. The teacher of this age group should realize the vast potential of the job experiences of the middle adult and seek to channel them into serving in some capacity in the local church.

For many in this age bracket, there is an increase in leisure time, especially when the kids are grown and moved out of the house. The middle adult should be challenged to manage his leisure time wisely and to investigate new ways to mentor others.

Often, the middle adult years are years of peak earning power and positions of leadership in the work place, the community, and the church. Stewardship of money and time should be stressed as well as the pitfalls of materialism. The middle adult should be encouraged to be an ethical and Christlike example to people in their workplace and community.

EMOTIONAL AND INTELLECTUAL CHARACTERISTICS

The middle adult years can bring the harsh reality of unfulfilled dreams and goals of young adulthood. One can easily punish themselves for past mistakes or "roads not taken". The middle adult needs to be reminded of the need to seek, find, and follow God's will in every area of life and to be future-focused instead of past-focused.

Often there is an unwillingness to learn new things and a strong resistance to change of any kind, especially if it is church-related. For the Sunday School teacher of middle adults the ministry of encouragement becomes very important. Middle adults need to be encouraged to expand their horizons mentally as they study the Scriptures and to get actively involved in the teaching-learning process.

The middle adult years often bring on stress related to teens in the home, the education of college-age children and the launching of those children into the world as young adults. Middle adult parents need the support of other Christians who are going through the same kinds of experiences and need the help of older adults who have lived through similar experiences. The teacher of middle adults should help them to focus on the opportunities of "letting go" of their children instead of the problems surrounding the process.

SPIRITUAL CHARACTERISTICS

Middle adults may awake to the reality that their life is half over resulting in a struggle with guilt over some past sin or failure. The truths of forgiveness of sins and release from guilt need to be emphasized.

Married couples may face the "empty nest syndrome" and need to continue to cultivate their relationship with each other. Couples need to re-establish areas of common interest and build their lives on each other instead of their children. The church can respond by providing the support of couples in similar situations and by continued teaching on the priority of the husband-wife relationship.

Since many in leadership positions in the church are middle adults, they are facing a time of spiritual burden bearing. This should be a time for increased dependence on the Lord for leadership in decision-making through the development of their prayer life and in-depth study of the Word of God. Teachers of middle adults should remind them of the need to maintain a high personal testimony as well as a spirit of compassion and understanding for the young adults who are working with them in the church.

The middle adult years should also be years of optimum service for the Lord and His church. Middle adults can usually be more successful in reaching other middle adults with the gospel then other age groups. They should be urged to take full advantage of evangelism opportunities. This becomes important to church growth in that often when a middle adult is won to Christ, his or her entire family will follow his lead.

MIDDLE ADULT LIFE TASKS

The teacher of middle adults needs to be aware of the major kinds of events that are happening in the lives of the average middle adult.

JOB—Change of job or job location, facing a job lay-off or unemployment, job dissatisfaction, job "burnout," choosing the time of retirement (early, normal, or late), widow facing the job market after years of absence from it.

AGING—Aging and sometimes parents failing in health, children leaving home, facing personal physical problems, new awareness of their own mortality.

FAMILY—Sometimes a "midlife" crisis, problems and changes in relationships with spouse, children and friends, parent-teen problems can be traumatic.

FINANCES—Spouses employment, providing for education of children, providing for retirement, providing for proper health care, facing a serious financial reversal.

All of these four areas have an impact on the daily life of the middle adult. They are all important to the middle adult and certainly effect their spiritual development as well. The teacher of middle adults should be aware of the need to build strong relationships inside and outside of the Sunday School or small group classroom.

MIDDLE ADULT PARANORMATIVE CRISES

Crisis is a part of life and Christians are certainly not exempt. The middle adult teacher should be aware of the kinds of crises that may occur in this age bracket and be ready to minister in these difficult situations.

DEATH OF A SPOUSE—This is never easy for anyone not even Christians to face, but it is certainly easier with the support and love of fellow believers. Perhaps the most difficult time is one or two weeks after the funeral when things begin to slow down and reality starts to set in. The Lord's grace is sufficient, but He often uses His people to be communicators and representatives of this grace.

DIVORCE—While not condoned by the church, divorce tragically is a reality and should be faced with compassion and understanding. A divorce situation does not exempt the church from the responsibility to minister to those who are affected by it. In many communities there are large numbers of divorced middle adults who feel completely cut-off from the ministry of a local church and who are waiting for someone who cares to reach out to them in love.

For those who have marriages that are shaky but not broken, the church needs to provide adequate counseling and instruction on how to keep the marriage together.

DEATH OF A CHILD—Certainly a time of great sorrow and distress, parents (and remaining siblings) need the special support of believers during this crisis. Often one or both parents will experience torment-ing guilt over the loss of a child. Parents who have been through similar circumstances can often be a tremendous help in the weeks and months following such an experience.

INCAPACITATING ILLNESS OF A SPOUSE, AGING PARENT, OR CHILD—Sometimes a prolonged, terminal illness (or condition) can be worse than death in the way that is can drain the inner resources of even the strongest believer. These middle adults need to be reminded of the all-sufficient grace of an all-loving and all-wise God. Again, other adults who have gone through similar circumstances can often offer counsel and support that can be unmatched by other sources. If a member of your class is the one who is seriously ill, consider recording in some manner the Sunday School lesson and having a member of the class take it by each week.

There are many other crises that are faced by some middle adults, but these are the major ones that you will confront in the average Sunday School or small group class.

SUGGESTIONS FOR MINISTRY TO MIDDLE ADULTS

Here are some ideas that may help you evaluate your current ministry with middle adults.

1. Determine the deep needs of the middle adults in your class. Offer suggestions as to specific reading materials dealing with problems that are commonly faced. Refer counseling for indi-viduals, couples, and families in need to your pastor or staff members.

2. Do all that you can to strengthen the family unit. Stress relationships that are based on Biblical guidelines between spouses as well as parents and children.

3. Give opportunities for Christian service and active involvement in the ministries of your church. Each middle adult should be involved directly in some type of ministry in your church.

4. Provide for times of relationship building and mutual support where middle adults can share with each other. Plan activities where the whole family can be together as well as times for adults only.

5. Do not shy away from the tough issues. Middle adults need to hear exactly what the Bible says on topics such as divorce, remarriage, childrearing, abortion, pornography, homosexuality, etc.

6. If you have a class that is exclusively middle adults, reach out socially to adults of other ages as well. The church is always stronger when various ages build closer relationships outside of class or the small group.

The middle adult years are years of growth, challenge and unprecedented spiritual opportunity. You, as a teacher, have an important responsibility to fulfill in meeting the spiritual needs of the middle adults under your care.

CHAPTER 13

CONCLUSION

IF YOU HAVE READ this far, you are dedicated to being the best teacher that your students deserve. Some would say it too much work to teach in your local church but many like you have committed to invest in students. As you walk your students up the six stairs of learning you will marvel at their spiritual maturity progress. Combining the six steps, the seven laws and the techniques found in this book will create a powerful and exciting learning environment for your Sunday School class or small group. The reason why you prepare each week is not to have the best lesson but to bring out the best in your students. Now go and teach students not lessons.

Dedicated to helping churches build strong
disciples, leaders and teachers.

For further information about the ministry of Evangelical Training
Association, call 800-369-8291 or visit www.etaworld.org.

THE RANDALL HOUSE
COMMENTARY SERIES

The *Randall House Bible Commentary* series is a must have for pastors and students alike. With Robert Picirilli as General Editor and all Free Will Baptist contributors, the *Randall House Bible Commentary* series is a great addition to any library.

$29.99 Each or All 8 for Only $199.99!

Mark *Picirilli*
ISBN 0892655003

John *Stallings*

ISBN 0892651377

1 and 2 Corinthians *Picirilli*

ISBN 0892659491

Galatians-Colossians *Marberry, Ellis, Picirilli*
ISBN 0892651342

1 Thessalonians- Philemon *Ellis, Outlaw, Picirilli*
ISBN 0892651431

Hebrews *Outlaw*
ISBN 0892655143

James, 1 and 2 Peter, Jude *Harrison, Picirilli*
ISBN 0892651458

To order call **1-800-877-7030** or visit our website at **www.RandallHouse.com**

NOTES